TWENTY IS PLENTY!

Growing Up as the Nineteenth Child
in a Family of Twenty Children

CAROL HAMPSON VISLOCKY

Edited by Linda Hampson Smedley.

Proofread by Richard Robinson.

Front Cover Image: Hampson Archives (unknown photographer)

Back Cover Image: Lindsay Flanagan Photography

Cover Design: Crystal Rothhaar

Printed in the United States of America.

ISBN: 1723384984
ISBN-13: 978-1723384981

CONTENTS

INTRODUCTION

As usual, I woke up early, dressed, and put on my sneakers to take my daily three-mile walk around scenic Rockland Lake. Unlike other mornings, I grabbed a pen and pad before I rushed out the door. As I walked and took in the natural beauty of the lake and its surroundings, I had the sudden urge to write, so I sat down at a picnic table and began journaling my childhood memories.

Eventually, I shared the notes with my daughter, Erica. She was enthusiastic about the idea of transferring my memories to paper. I appreciated her support.

A few weeks after my inspirational walk my sister, Linda, visited from Maine. Erica excitedly had me share my notes with her Aunt Linda. Linda shared her vision that this had the makings of a book and offered to assist in telling my story. Her confidence in me that I could write a story in my own words helped this book to eventually become a reality.

While working on it, we were recalling positive and negative memories. We stopped when they became too emotional for us to express. Years later a third family reunion was planned for 2018 and inspired me to return to writing.

Some of our siblings shared their thoughts of past events with us. Naturally, we did not always recall events the same way. I have done my best to put into words their recollections as they were communicated to me. Ultimately, this book is based on my memories and told from my perspective of growing up as the nineteenth child of my parents, Harold and Inez Hampson.

My story begins with Erica's wedding and a dream come true.

CHAPTER ONE

A DREAM COME TRUE

My husband, Peter Vislocky, and I had one child from our union. As a proud mother, I begin my story sharing memories of Erica's wedding. For over a year she and I planned her big day. I am known for being a very pragmatic person. The practical thing to have done would have been to give Erica a large sum of money for a down payment on a house and pay for a modest wedding. However, I have inherited my mother's romantic side. Though very poor at times in my life, I grew to love and respect the finer things. I desired these things for Erica. Thus, a fairy tale wedding. She had the experience of Cinderella attending the ball. With the help of John's parents and Erica's grandmother, Peter's mother, this was a classy wedding.

In planning the event, we wanted to meet Erica and John's expectations of a perfect wedding. We also desired to surpass the expectations of those relatives and guests who would be traveling far distances to attend. Our hope was that each guest would enjoy partaking in this fairy tale, and they did.

When the big day, October 9, 2010, finally arrived, the sun was shining, the October sky was clear and sparkling blue. The temperature was just right - not too hot, not too cold. We arrived at St. Anthony's Church with love in our hearts. My daughter and her fiancé had been together for a few years and they formed a deep abiding love for one another. They were married by a priest in the company of many relatives and friends who deeply loved them.

I walked down the aisle on my brother Jesse's arm. This was so appropriate since it was he who walked me down the aisle when I was married; my dad was deceased at the time. We walked proudly with our heads held high and our hearts united on this special occasion.

The "Bridal Chorus" played as Erica marched down the aisle on the arm of her father. They were striking to behold; she was tall with long blonde ringlet curls draping down her shoulders. Her figure was so perfect that she could have been on the cover of a magazine. Yet, she was our daughter with a heart more precious than her outside beauty could ever express. Erica was a vision. She appeared as an angel from heaven with an aura emanating from her. Through her long, beautiful veil, I could see that she was smiling and filled with joy. Never had I seen my husband so solemn, so proud, and so handsome. Oh, what a happy day! The future was hers and John's, with God's blessing from above.

After the wedding, there was a reception held in Garrison, New York. They walked down the stone pathway lined with magnificent maple and pine trees to the elegant country venue. After entering through French doors that led to a cozy foyer, family and friends proceeded into an elegant rustic room. Here many of the married couples viewed pictures of themselves as they appeared on their own wedding day. Afterwards, they entered onto a colossal terrace overlooking the Hudson River Valley. They enjoyed drinks and hors d'oeuvres while socializing before entering the romantically candlelit ballroom to enjoy the rest of the celebration.

During the wedding reception, I stepped outside where I encountered my nephew, Roland. We talked about the wedding. A moment occurred when I became overwhelmed by the luxury and elegance of everything: the beauty of my daughter, the exquisite décor of the venue, the place settings, the sunflower and roses centerpieces and the gaiety of the music. Suddenly, I was transported back to being the poor little girl who lived on

Congers Road in an old broken-down house. I remembered how I felt freezing cold as I wore a coat in the house because there was no heat. The shame and embarrassment that I felt wearing ragged hand-me-down clothes to school. I never imagined that poor little girl would grow up one day to provide her daughter with a far more comfortable lifestyle. Yet, here I stood at the fairy tale wedding I provided for my daughter. How did this poor little girl acquire the styles and tastes of the rich? As I spoke with Roland, a great sense of pride swept over me. My dream of a spectacular wedding for my daughter had come true. It was one of the best days of my life!

CHAPTER TWO

THE BEGINNING

Harold and Inez Hampson gave my brother Roy the privilege of naming me Carol. I reflect on my life's journey as their nineteenth child.

My father, Harold Edward Hampson, graduated in 1930 from West Warwick High School in West Warwick, Rhode Island. When he was in high school, his yearbook described him as "Everybody's friend. He is a good sport, not only figuratively but also athletically. With a radiant personality, a magnetic knack of making real friends of all his acquaintances. Harold should not be bothered by the fight." His class honored him by giving him a class gift: "Pinky, our class could not be complete without a 'Redhead'; so in case you grow bald, use this red paint on the roof. (Red paint)." He was 18 years old when he started dating Inez Rathbun. Upon learning she was pregnant, just three weeks shy of her sixteenth birthday, the couple married on May 9, 1931, in West Warwick, Rhode Island. With a twinkle in her eye and an endearing smile on her face, she loved telling everyone, "It was love at first sight when I first saw Harold." Their love affair was to continue for the rest of their married lives and lasted more than thirty-nine years, until Mama's death.

Daddy's father, Edward Hampson, "Grandpa Ted," was born June 6, 1886 in Long Eaton, Derbyshire, England. He was a quiet man with a gentle soul. He became a lace weaver, a much-respected trade. Grandpa Ted was about 5 feet 8 inches tall but we always looked up to him as a giant. He had such a great appreciation for the beauty of flowers. People would stop by his house and admire his magnificent landscape designs.

Daddy's mother Annie Maria Mee, "Grandma Hampson," was born March 10, 1888 in Belton, England. She was a true-blue English-bred woman. Her hair was naturally golden blonde and hung to her waist but she usually wore it in a bun. She had an appreciation for huge, beautiful hats adorned with colorful flowers, feathers, and ribbons. She was known for wearing high-quality clothes and kept up with the fashion of the day.

Grandma Hampson and Grandpa Ted married on August 3, 1907 in The Parish Church of Loughborough, Leicester, England. They emigrated to the United States from Liverpool, England on the vessel Franconia. They arrived at the port of Boston, Massachusetts on or about July 18, 1911. They resided at Maple Avenue, Phenix, Rhode Island. It is here he continued his trade as a lace weaver, which provided them with a comfortable lifestyle. He was employed by Phenix Lace Mill and Bancroft Lace Company for a total of 41 years. In addition, he spent five years employed by Linwood Lace Works in Washington, Rhode Island. Daddy would continue this strong work ethic modeled by Grandpa Ted.

Grandma Hampson and Grandpa Ted were special to me. They seemed so prim and proper. They continued to practice many English traditions in America. Every day they would have a set time to eat, drink tea and take naps.

My paternal grandparents were blessed with three children: Harold "Daddy", Dolsie, and Norman.

Daddy was born September 8, 1912, in Riverpoint, Rhode Island. I remember seeing a photograph of him as a little boy with long hair past his shoulders and wearing an elaborate lace dress, and tights. It is difficult to tell in that photograph if he was a boy or a girl. It was a sign of the times! Daddy was a true American patriot! When the U.S. government called for men to serve as soldiers in World War II, he was devastated when he was turned down because he suffered from asthma. He had a great appreciation of music and had a passion for dancing.

Jesse Clifford Rathbun, Mama's father "Grandpa Jess", was born on February 15, 1892 in Voluntown, Connecticut. Since I was too young to remember Grandpa Jess, the memories I share of him have been verbally passed down to me. He earned his living as a lineman. He climbed forty-foot poles where he repaired electrical outages and restored electricity to the community. Besides working on fair weather days, he was called upon to work through hurricanes, thunderstorms, and ice storms. The most amazingly verified story passed down through the years is how he was accidentally jolted with 4,000 volts of electricity while repairing wires in an ice storm. He miraculously lived through it! "The fact that he survived the 4,000-volt shock was amazing, considering that most executioners use only half that, 2,000 volts, to kill a man in the electric chair", stated one of the newspaper articles.[1] This "shocking" event in no way deterred him from returning to climbing poles no matter the weather conditions. He retired when he was 65.

Mama's mother, Edith May Brown, was born on July 6, 1895 in Washington, Rhode Island. She was known as "Grandma Rathbun" and loved socializing. She actively supported and served in her community. She also told fortunes using a crystal ball, which has been passed down to one of her grandsons. In one newspaper article, there is a picture of Grandma reading tarot cards. "Mme. Swalli Rathboneski (Mrs. Edith Rathbun to her friends and neighbors) tells Luther Capwell's fortune at the Riverpoint Fire Department's 'Klondike Nights.' The three-night event is being held to raise money for fire fighting equipment."[2] Also, at one time she was the new noble grand of Mary Rebekah Lodge, 100F. She enjoyed gambling; she attended bingo halls, where she chatted with family, friends, and people in the community, and where she competed to win jackpots. Mama went to the bingo with her. Could it be this is the genesis of our

---

[1] Litner, Jerry. "He Took a Jolt of 4,000 Volts and Now Scales Poles Again." *Providence Sunday Journal*. 16 January, Year Unknown. Hampson Family Archives.

[2] "Klondike Nights" in Another Arctic." Newspaper Unknown. Date Unknown. Hampson Family Archives.

family interest in gambling?

Grandma did not pay any attention to what other people thought of her. Back in the day, it was considered unladylike and sinful for a woman to smoke cigarettes; she did it anyway! Unfortunately, a time came when she suffered so severely from arthritis that she was unable to walk. When I was a little girl she came to live with us for awhile. She became bedridden and a bed had to be brought downstairs and placed in the parlor for her. The highlight of her day was having Linda wash and curl her hair. The joints in her fingers and hands became so deformed that it was difficult for her to move them. She could no longer smoke, but she did find a way to use snuff. I enjoyed playing cards with Grandma; we usually would play for a nickel a game. The only problem was that I would cheat. Grandma would call me on it sometimes, but of course I would always deny it when she and Mama would question me about it. I still wonder why the heck I wanted to cheat at cards with this sweet dear old woman. Well, come to think of it, I guess I was quite a "ticket" myself at times, just like Grandma.

Grandpa and Grandma Rathbun married and had four children: Inez Elizabeth, Pauline, Charles (a Sergeant in the United States Army Air Force during WW II), and Raymond (who served in the U.S. Army). Grandma Rathbun and Grandpa Jess were very proud grandparents. They took an interest in their grandchildren's high academic successes and their sports accomplishments.

Inez Elizabeth Rathbun "Mama," was born on May 30, 1915 in Fiskeville (Scituate), Rhode Island. I discovered that her genealogy dated back to the early settlers of Block Island, Rhode Island. This history has served as a great sense of pride for the Rathbun family.

Mama was very intelligent and even skipped a grade in school. Despite having been an excellent student, Mama dropped out of school when she was only 15 years of age – a mere child when she married and became a mother. She was approximately 5 feet three inches tall. She was considered a stunning dark-haired beauty as a young woman. She had a shapely figure and accentuated it by wearing glamorous clothes. Besides having been a meticulous dresser, she drew much gratification from wearing her hair in the popular styles of the day. Mama had a contagious laugh and was full of fun. However, her sunny disposition was dampened whenever there was a thunderstorm. Apparently, an event occurred that traumatized her to fear them. This phobia persisted throughout the rest of her life. She also had a fear of flying. Her favorite pastime was dancing with Daddy. The young couple earned the respect and admiration of the dance hall crowds, as they gracefully flowed across the floor. Often, they won top prize in dance competitions.

CHAPTER THREE

THE BOND IS CREATED

During the 1930's, it was not unusual for people to marry at a young age and to have large families. However, I am sure my parents could not have imagined what the future held for them when they began their life's journey together. Certainly, they never could have imagined that they would have twenty children (twelve boys and eight girls) over a period of nearly twenty-six years. Mama had all single births.

The order, from the oldest to the youngest, is as follows:

	Name	Birth Date	Death Date
1	Harold Edward	November 13, 1931	February 4, 1932
2	Edith May	January 24, 1933	December 17, 2014
3	Edward Clifford	April 3, 1934	October 13, 2013
4	Harry Lee	June 8, 1935	September 3, 2012
5	Donald Jesse	August 11, 1936	April 27, 2011
6	Inez	November 16, 1937	
7	Roy Charles	December 11, 1938	January 30, 2002
8	Norman William	December 5, 1939	May 22, 1950
9	Roland	January 28, 1941	May 22, 1950
10	Charles Raymond	June 10, 1943	
11	Baby Girl	April 17, 1944	April 18, 1944
12	Annie Maria Mee	May 7, 1945	
13	Jesse Clifford	May 6, 1946	August 16, 2013
14	Robert Carl	August 7, 1947	October 13, 1996
15	David Roger	July 10, 1948	February 10, 2013
16	Linda Nancy	January 29, 1950	
17	Ruth Ellen	January 12, 1952	April 8, 2017
18	Judith Karen	May 31, 1953	
19	Carol Ann	July 28, 1954	
20	Marvin Lester	April 16, 1957	February 20, 2014

In the beginning of their marriage Daddy held menial jobs. Eventually, Daddy earned an excellent salary working as a lace weaver to support what was initially a small family. Life was very good for this young couple, especially when their first child, my father's namesake, Harold Edward, was born, making them a happy family of three. Grandparents and family members doted on Harold, but then the unimaginable happened. One day Mama went to check on her first-born child in his crib. He was dead. Baby Harold's death occurred on February 4, 1932, when he was two months and twenty one days old. His cause of death was probably thymus disease (disease of the thymus gland). Erroneously, some held the young parents responsible for the unexpected death of their infant due to their own lack of knowledge about thymus death. The pain my parents suffered was inconceivable. Daddy was only nineteen. Mama was only sixteen and only a child herself. Can you imagine experiencing something so earth shattering when you yourself are still a child? Though the memory of the unbearable pain of Harold's death would lessen over time, Harold would live in their hearts forever. Living through their overwhelming loss contributed to the formation of a bond between them no man could tear asunder. Did my parents subconsciously compensate for their loss by having such a large family? We never knew.

On January 24, 1933, my parents were blessed with their second child, Edith. She brought the young couple great joy and helped them to move past the nightmarish loss of their beloved first son. Their lives moved forward, and Mama would give birth to eight more children: Edward, Harry, Donald, Inez, Roy, Norman, Roland, and Charlie.

When Mama was seven months pregnant with her 11th child, tragedy struck again. Her baby girl was born premature and only lived for four hours. Once again, my parents' love for each other would get them through the heart-wrenching pain of losing another baby. As time went on Mama would give birth to her next five children: Annie, Jesse, Bobby, David, and Linda.

Life would not remain peaceful for this large family. Unimaginable tragedy loomed on the horizon.

CHAPTER FOUR

TRAGEDY AT THE LAKE

The family home was within walking distance of Lake Tiogue in Coventry, Rhode Island. My brothers Roland, 9, and Norman, 10, accidentally drowned in the lake on May 22, 1950. Their drowning was a shocking and monumental loss to our family.

Occasionally, people would question me about how they died. It was very difficult to respond because I was not there. I was not born until four years after this tragedy occurred. I do not recall my parents ever sharing the details of this horrific accident. I have memories of my older brothers and sisters sharing bits and pieces about it. Also, I remember viewing photos of my brothers in their coffins, but I could not bear looking at them. Viewing the photos literally made me feel sick. It was a common practice for relatives to photograph their deceased loved ones back then. I am glad that my family does not practice this ritual any longer.

While visiting my cousin Brian Rathbun, the topic of my brothers' deaths arose, and he provided me with copies of newspaper articles about their drowning. According to the articles, Roland and Norman were playing with a group of boys, which included two of their brothers, on a part of Lake Tiogue called Pirate Den Point. Roland and Norman jumped onto a makeshift raft. They panicked when the raft started drifting too far away from shore; they slid off the raft into "the cold, choppy lake waters" and started swimming back to shore.[3] While they were very good swimmers, it was believed that the cold water caused them to cramp up and left them incapable of swimming.

Two of their brothers, Donald and Roy, got into an old rowboat and attempted to reach them, but the boat sank. Donald, 13 and Roy, 11 had to be rescued themselves. Fortunately, one of the boys from the group informed an adult of the crisis developing at the lake. The police and fire departments arrived. While some rescue workers were attempting to resuscitate Roland and Norman, others rescued Donald and Roy who were discovered floating on the same raft from which Roland and Norman had slid off.

While writing this book, my brothers Jesse and Charlie shared some memories with me. Jesse said, "I was four years old when this tragedy happened. I remember Daddy coming home from work. Many rescue personnel were at the lake trying to save the boys. Mama was holding Linda (three months old) in her arms on the front steps. Everything was very chaotic. I was there when the boys were pronounced dead. Mama had to be sedated." My brother Charlie shared this memory; he did not talk for months after the tragedy. He believed that this was the beginning of his stuttering problem.

Mama endured the heartache of losing her children for the rest of her life. As a child, I remember coming home from school and seeing Mama crying while sitting in her parlor chair. When I asked her why she was crying, she told me that it was because she was thinking about my brothers who drowned. She told me not to tell anyone that she had been crying. She did not want anyone to know the depth of her sorrow. I felt Mama's pain that day. She desperately missed her sons. It made me wish I had known my brothers, Roland and Norman. I had kept her secret all these years and now share this memory today because the little girl inside me wishes I had known the right thing to say and could have wiped away her tears.

---

[3] "Two Youthful Brothers Drown at Lake Tiogue When Their Raft Sinks." *Pawtuxet Valley Daily Times* [West Warwick, RI], 23 May 1950, 59(254). Hampson Family Archives.

CHAPTER FIVE

TWENTY IS PLENTY

Mama and Daddy held the family together after the absolutely devastating loss of their two sons. There was great sadness in our family. Knowing their remaining children needed their love and guidance, they found the strength to continue raising them. Time marched on and Mama gave birth to three more children in Rhode Island: Ruthie, Judy, and Carol.

The lace mill where Daddy worked closed. Daddy was out of work. In 1956 Mama was pregnant and they moved with nine of their children from Coventry, Rhode Island to Westwood, New Jersey. My other siblings had established their independence. Daddy became employed again as a lace weaver. This was a major move. Mama and Daddy ventured into unknown territory with nine kids in tow. How would the children adjust to living in a new environment must have been foremost in their minds. I was a toddler at the time and have no memories of it. However, I can't begin to imagine how my parents managed to move: mattresses, box springs, bed frames, appliances, and that's not all! Dressers, tables, chairs, dishes, pots and pans, and clothing for 11 people. Family members traveled the long journey by car. Cars! No seatbelts! No GPS! Roads were not what they are today! Trips took longer simply based on the fact that speed limits were lower than today. How many bathroom stops? How many times did they hear, "Are we there yet?" How many times did they repeat "Behave yourselves back there"? They moved a couple more times before they finally settled down once and for all. Phew!

The year 1957 was an eventful year. The Hampson family moved from Westwood, New Jersey to East Orange, New Jersey. I have no memory of living in East Orange. Inez was a young adult in 1957, so Linda and I called her to ask if there were any memories she would like to share. When Inez lived at home she helped take care of the younger children. She was the "go to" person when there was a crisis. She stated, "Okay, it was Marvin's birth and I came home. I left college because at Christmas time I saw that Mama was having trouble with her pregnancy. I was at home when she started her labor. Mama told me to call your father and tell him to come home, that it is time for the birth of the baby (we didn't have a telephone so all calls were made at a pay phone). I went and did what she told me. I stayed with her until Daddy came home and took her to the hospital." Daddy drove Mama to Nyack Hospital in Nyack, New York. (I do not know why they went to a New York hospital when they lived in New Jersey.) While at the hospital, "Mama had a rabbit test; rabbit test came back negative that she was not pregnant. That doctor thought she had a tumor. I remember Mama said, 'I know I'm pregnant. I know I'm having a baby. It wasn't a tumor." Mama was right!

Inez continued, "I remember when my siblings had come home from school I gathered them all around and told them Daddy had taken Mama to the hospital. I said a prayer. We were all praying for Mama to get better; and Bobby jumped up and said, 'No, I don't want to say this prayer. Mama's not coming home and she's not going to get better.' He ran upstairs screaming, and I had to comfort him."

She added, "Mama was probably in the hospital for two weeks. The reason she was in the hospital was not so much because she was in labor, but that her blood pressure was 280 (very high). Marvin was the only caesarean birth that Mama had." Mama was 41 years old when she gave birth to her twentieth child. Due to the circumstances of Mama's health, the doctor delivered her premature baby by caesarean section. Marvin was born! Mama then had her tubes tied. Even though my parents were so young having twenty children they accepted and believed they were gifts from God. That gave them the strength to be able to go on and deal with the difficulties they had in their lives. Twenty is Plenty!

CHAPTER SIX

A FRESH START

In 1957 the Hampson family made its final move from East Orange, New Jersey to Congers Road in New City, New York. My parents leased an old Victorian-style house from the Starkes. They weren't only our landlords, they were Donald's in-laws. He married their daughter Marion. The move to New City provided my parents with a fresh outlook on life.

Mama and Daddy were more comfortable and happier now than they had been for some time. New City was a great place to raise a family. It provided a first-class education at nearby schools. Next door to our house were dairy farms which offered a simpler way of life while the multi-cultural world of New York City was a thirty-minute drive away.

This house is the place Mama and Daddy chose for us to learn about being a close-knit family. As long as there is love there is hope, and we could conquer whatever obstacles came our way. Mama loved this house! It was spacious and charming. It is here where a house finally became our home. While it is important to remember my deceased siblings, it was in this house where we became known as a family of 16 children.

We were just settling into the house when my parents hosted a 50th Wedding Anniversary party for Grandma Hampson and Grandpa Ted on August 3, 1957. I have a vivid memory of being in the dining room of this house at their party when I was three years old. Family members were laughing and celebrating this joyous occasion.

An old wooden piano was in the parlor when we moved into the house. Daddy would play the piano and I have warm memories of sitting next to him on the piano bench. I thought the songs he played sounded beautiful. I later learned the piano was out of tune, which is probably why he didn't play it very often. Eventually the piano was thrown out.

Daddy was a quiet man, though I wish I had paid more attention when he shared his thoughts. I do recollect him saying, "Don't burn your bridges. You never know when you will go back over that bridge again." Daddy possessed a love of history. As a little girl, Daddy took me on a day trip to visit the Empire State Building and the Statue of Liberty in New York City. I believe this was an attempt by him to encourage me to develop an interest in the historical landmarks. At the time I couldn't have cared less about such things. He always watched the news and read the newspaper. His interest in current events and world and local news must have had an impact on me. As an adult I try to keep well-informed of current events. Daddy had poor health. He suffered with asthma and diabetes throughout his life. He had difficulty breathing and would use his inhaler to get relief. His diabetes caused him to drink at least a gallon of water a day. Later in life his diabetes became life-threatening.

Mama was a homemaker.. She wore house dresses around the house, but she did love to dress up to go to weddings and other special occasions. I especially remember that Linda curled her hair for these events. She was proud of how she looked in her new dresses! She was a great nurturer, and whenever anyone in the house got sick, she would offer comforting words and provide an over-the-counter medicine (Stanback) to fix the hurt. I recall Linda having walking pneumonia. She was so sick and stayed upstairs in bed with a high fever. Even though Mama rarely went upstairs because it was difficult for her to go up and down the steep narrow wooden stairs she went up there to take care of her. She had a bowl of water and a face cloth and kept wiping her forehead to help lower the fever. She gave Linda the love and care she needed to get better. Mama was so unusual in that she could love twenty children and treat each one as if they were the only one.

At times there were disagreements among us. No one wanted anyone else telling them what to do. When Mama was home and we argued so much she needed a break. She would go outside and sit in the car until her nerves calmed down. I don't know how she did it!

After having so many children, Mama put on a considerable amount of weight. Her weight gain was possibly caused by her thyroid disease. She had an operation to remove a goiter. The doctor cut her neck from one side to the other leaving a huge long scar. High blood pressure would be a problem the rest of her life.

She did not drive, which bothered me because most of my friends' mothers did. Mama was very close to Pauline (Eddie's wife). She treated her like a daughter as Pauline's parents lived in Rhode Island. She would drive Mama around so she could complete her errands (shopping, paying bills, etc.). When she took her to pick up Daddy's paycheck a few of us would also go. Sometimes after cashing his check at the bank we would go to a nearby inexpensive restaurant for lunch where they had great specials. A huge treat for us! This was Mama's way of thanking Pauline for driving her around.

When Mama had a few extra dollars she enjoyed going to the bingo. This was her form of entertainment. Sometimes she would take me or one or more of my siblings to the bingo with her. She also took us to the race track a few times. This was more fun for me than going to the bingo. I especially enjoyed watching Mama's face when she won. My favorite form of gambling is playing blackjack in the casino. Sometimes I wish Mama could be sitting right next to me at a blackjack table enjoying the thrill of playing the game with me. I'd love to see the expression on her face now as she walked through the exciting atmosphere of a casino. We would have so much fun together.

Gambling became part of many of our lives right into

adulthood. I know that it draws negative responses. Everyone spends their money on something and I don't tell them how to spend their money. I look at this as my entertainment. I am a moderate gambler who, like Mama, enjoys the thrill of winning. I am not condoning gambling for other people. Of course gambling has a losing side. I don't like losing but when I gamble I'm willing to risk losing in order to enjoy the thrill of the game. As adults my siblings, nieces, nephews and I go gambling together. For us it is time spent having fun.

Religion played a big part in the Hampson household. I believe that it served as a foundation for my family. Our prayers were said nightly asking the Lord to bless Mama, Daddy, naming all our siblings, and others involved in our lives. My parents had passionate beliefs about how their children should be raised, and rarely swayed from those beliefs. There were rules to follow and obey without question and expectations to be met. Schoolwork, chores, and extracurricular activities were to be performed to the best of our abilities. Arriving late to any planned event was unacceptable. Punctuality was a must. Even to this day, I make a point of not being late for social and professional commitments. We were taught to be happy for each other's individual successes. Jealousy was not tolerated. When one did well, it was a reflection upon our entire family. Good manners (like "please and thank you" and "Mr. and Mrs.") were also instilled in the family. They were superstitious! We were told to never put new shoes on the table, never break a mirror, and never walk under a ladder. They put fear into us that if we did any of these things we would have bad luck. Judy and I remember they would always say "knock on wood" to prevent bad luck from happening. Judy says it to this day!

I'm sure if you asked any Hampson they would tell you chowder and clam cakes were a big part of our lives growing up. Occasionally, we would take day trips visiting our relatives in Rhode Island. While visiting, there were times when we would eat at Rocky Point in Warwick, Rhode Island. They had a huge dinner hall in which they had a reasonably priced meal for kids to eat. We delighted in eating chowder, clam cakes, sweet corn and watermelon. If we weren't eating chowder in Rhode Island, Daddy enjoyed making chowder for our family at home. Every time I eat chowder out I compare it to his. I always say Daddy's was the best!

CHAPTER SEVEN

FUN TIMES

The house was situated on a dangerous curve. In front of the house was a lawn where I played ball with my siblings. Aware of the dangerous curve and the lawn being so close to the road, Mama would get upset with us and tell us to go play in the backyard. She feared we would run out into the road and get hit by a car. She did not want to lose any more children.

On the lawn was a flagpole. Daddy would hang a flag on it. It was extremely important to him to follow the national protocol of the handling of the flag.

We would get excited when we heard the music of the Good Humor truck coming down the road and turning into our driveway. We would dash into the house where Mama gave us money to buy ice cream. Sadly, I recall times when Mama did not have any money to give us, so we could not buy ice cream. I remember Judy and me looking under the cushions of Mama's parlor chair and couch for any money that may have fallen between them.

There were steps that sat near the road with a cement walkway that led up to the house. I remember sitting on these steps with Mama and Judy waiting for her school bus to arrive. Judy was age 5 and in kindergarten. I was 4 years old and would burst into tears because I also wanted to go on the school bus. Eventually the day came when I would ride the school bus.

Instead of feeling excited and happy to climb aboard the bus, I did not want to get on it! I wanted to stay at home with Mama. Now I realize that I was suffering from separation anxiety. I believe this experience so traumatized me that attending school became a problem for me.

The cement walkway was lined with tall hedges on both sides. Bobby taught me how to trim the hedges. They were so tall that I had to stand on something to trim them with hedge shears. They would take hours to finish. It was a very labor-intensive job that I shall never forget. It was too big a job for me as a little girl to handle!

Right past the hedges were steps that led up to the oversized outside porch with wooden pillars. Marvin, Judy, and I loved playing on the porch. We would play hopscotch, jump rope, jacks, pickup sticks, and all kinds of ball games for hours.

From the porch we could see the majestic maple tree standing in the front yard. Mama would love sitting on the porch with her children as the sweet smell of the lilac bushes drifted over when the wind blew.

We especially enjoyed being on the porch when it was raining. Of course, when it was thundering and lightning Mama called us into the house.

When Grandpa Ted came to visit we would sit on our front porch and he would lovingly share his stories about his life growing up in England. I did not pay much attention back then, and now I am so sorry for that. As an adult I wished he had written those stories down. I believe this is when a seed was planted for the writing of my memoir. While holding my hand we would take strolls around our property and he would tell me the names of the flowers. When I had a home of my own I would come to enjoy gardening. I lined my driveway with colorful arrays of flowers.

Sometimes I would see Daddy tossing out stale bread to feed the birds. I remember when he would hand the bread to me or one of my siblings so we could feed the birds as well. It is a memory I hold dear to my heart.

In the back of the house was a beautiful expansive yard. I can still recall that sweet smell of cut grass after Bobby mowed it. He even took the time to teach me how to mow. To the right of the back door was a narrow path that led to a small, charming, hedge enclosed, stone patio with a wooden frame that had plump green grapes hanging from it. On the adjoining property there was an elongated building that Bobby used as a chicken coop. Bobby and David turned it into a clubhouse for awhile. They were the joint presidents of the club. Linda, Ruthie, Judy, and I were the only other members. Inviting us to be members of their club was such an honor for us. They called the meetings together following Robert's Rules of Order and conducted the club just like professionals. They had learned about Robert's Rules in school. The Little Rascals had nothing over us when it came to having fun. Bobby raised chickens and turkeys for awhile. He gave the turkeys names and became very attached to them. When Ruthie was quite young she noticed one of the chickens appeared to be sick. She took it out of the pen and brought it into the kitchen. She turned the oven on and placed the sick chicken in it. She was hoping the heat would make it better. A very short time passed when she realized the chicken might get cooked and die. Oops!

I had fun-filled times playing with my siblings. Since we did not have any sand, we sifted and played with dirt. Sometimes we built forts together. I especially enjoyed when we played kick ball, baseball, or basketball. One of the best aspects of being a part of a large family was that we always had enough of us to make a complete team. The barn at the top of the driveway was where we would play basketball. Marvin would practice for hours. Judy and I delighted in climbing trees. As little girls it seemed we would sit up there for hours at a time. When the sun blazed down on us, Marvin, Judy, and I had great fun running under a hose to cool off. In the evening we fancied catching lightning bugs in the dark. Such happy times!

A large field stretched between our house and our landlord's, the Starkes. They owned the dairy farm next door. Barbed wire fencing separated the field from Starke's pasture, which sloped down a steep hill. It was here the cows and bull would graze.

They had ponies (Lucky, Daisy, and One Spot) that we would ride. In the winter my siblings and I would sleigh down the hill. It was especially beautiful to sleigh ride under the winter moonlight that shined down on the hill. Nothing was better than having our own private hill to sled down! Since there was only one sled, we would use anything that was available to us; an old tire, a piece of plywood, or the flying saucers received as Christmas gifts. It was thrilling to ride down on David's, Bobby's, or Jesse's back. Who could go the furthest without ending up in the cold brook at the bottom of the hill? After rushing home at the end of the day, Mama would be waiting to hear all about our thrilling adventures. We ran into the house freezing because we used socks for our mittens and we didn't have snow boots, only sneakers on our feet. Everyone would remove their wet clothes and hang them on the tall radiators throughout the house. Those radiators were a godsend. They would also warm our hands and feet. Only then could we relax, sip hot chocolate, and most of all enjoy being together.

These are happy memories I have cherished through the years. This was a time of innocence, such a playful time! Of course, I had no idea what the future held for my family. Like Mama often sang, "Que será, será - Whatever will be, will be."

CHAPTER EIGHT

FIRE! FIRE!

Our house had a glass-enclosed porch which brings back memories of a significant incident that occurred in 1958. One day, when I was four years old, I was at home with three of my siblings: Judy, 5, Ruthie, 6, and Charlie, 15. Mama had gone out with Marion to run some errands. Mama left Charlie to babysit us. While Charlie had gone upstairs and Ruthie was in the living room, Judy and I had gotten a hold of some matches and a pencil. We went out on the porch and sat down on a pile of clothes on the cement floor. We lit a match and tried to light the pencil tip. The match was dropped because it was too hot to handle, falling onto Judy's pants. We then realized that her pants had caught on fire (back then, children's clothes were not flame retardant). We started screaming, "Fire! Fire!" Charlie and Ruthie heard all the hysteria and came running onto the porch. Charlie extinguished the fire. Judy was screaming in pain and Charlie ran, carrying her to the bathtub where he put cold water on her leg. Soon after Mama came home and became frantic upon learning that Judy's leg was burned. Marion immediately drove Mama and Judy to the office of our family physician, Dr. Rich. Judy was then taken to the hospital. Her leg was so severely burned that the doctor was not sure if he was going to be able to save it. Because of the excellent care she was given, her leg was saved and she ended up with a six inch scar. Judy stayed in the hospital for at least a month. Mama thought Dr. Rich was a saint for saving Judy's leg.

After Judy came home from the hospital, Miss Stevens, her kindergarten teacher, came to visit her. She brought her lots of cards and gifts from children and parents. Miss Steven's act of kindness may have influenced Judy to become a kindergarten teacher later in life. Sadly, I do not think I cried at the time because I was jealous of all the attention she received.

Judy and I had never spoken again about the fire until I called her a few years ago. She told me she started the fire and not me. I did not believe her. We both believed we had started the fire. She said, "I told you it wasn't you. You got the blame for it, but it was really I who started the fire." After hanging up the phone with her I asked myself why I remembered being the one holding the match. I blamed myself and lived with the guilt all of these years for hurting her. I realized I had suppressed my feelings because the pain was too hard to handle. In writing this story, I am now able to cry about that terrible day. No matter who started the fire, we were both in on it. She has also had to live with this her whole life. We were just children who were being mischievous. We were fortunate we did not burn the house down.

CHAPTER NINE

HARDSHIPS

The Hampson family's comfortable standard of living was soon to become one of extreme hardship. After World War II, the American lace trade was drastically affected when America began importing lace from foreign countries. Many American lace mills were unable to compete with the foreign markets due to the low price of lace they could afford to charge. Daddy worked in a mill in New York City as a highly skilled lace weaver which, unfortunately, shut down. Due to no fault of his own, he lost his job. The harsh reality of Daddy being out of work was that there was no money coming in. Daddy loved being a tradesman. It was a major part of his identity, the foundation of his manhood. The rug had been pulled out from under him and he walked the streets to try to find work. Since he was unable to find work he had to give up his trade. The two years it took to find work were very tough on him and our family. We became financially impoverished. With only a high school education he would need to work two full-time jobs hoping to make ends meet. Hard work was second nature to him. Daddy eventually worked at Nyack Hospital in the boiler room for a time. Another job he had was as a machinist at the Dexter Company in Pearl River, New York and he was also employed as a custodian for the County of Rockland, New City, New York. Daddy would pass down the same high work expectations he learned from Grandpa Ted to his own children.

Mama and Daddy scraped together every penny they had to support us and to pay the bills. There was not enough income to feed our family. The food bill was enormous with so many people to feed. My parents needed help making ends meet.

As small children, my brothers (aged 9-13) worked as caddies. It was backbreaking work for them at such a young age. My brothers' hard-earned money helped to support the household. They worked weekends and on school holidays. David, Bobby, Jesse, and Charlie would leave the house before 7 A.M. and not arrive home until nightfall after caddying at Spring Rock Country Club. They were pressured to caddy as many loops (i.e., rounds of golf) as possible. Throughout the summer months, they worked in the blistering heat. Charlie attended school during the day, caddied on the weekends, and worked nights at the A&P Supermarket. They would find other odd jobs such as shoveling driveways in the winter months. My brothers felt it was unfair they had to work and miss out on a normal childhood. They had every right to feel this way. It was definitely a very sad situation.

When Mama had the money to buy food she would have dinner ready on the table when Daddy and my brothers came home from work. She was a great cook, like Grandma Rathbun. My favorites were torpedo sauce, butterscotch candy, baked apples with cinnamon, rhubarb pie and peanut butter fudge. The girls had to help with household chores. Mama shopped at A&P for her groceries and we had to carry tons of grocery bags from the car into the house. It was feast or famine. When Mama went food shopping, our refrigerator and cabinets were full. It seemed by the next day all the food was gone.

So many dishes, pots, and pans to clean! We did not have a dishwasher. Can you imagine how many dishes there were to wash, dry, and put away? It was like working in a restaurant kitchen, yet this was our everyday life. Sometimes, when I did the dishes all by myself, I talked to myself and created a pretend friend to keep me company because it was so lonely and boring.

So much laundry! For a short while we had an old fashioned washing machine and dried our clothes on a clothes line. When we did not have a washing machine we washed our clothes by hand. We hung them to dry in the bathroom and over dining room and kitchen chairs. Because the clothes were often still wet in the morning we would have to resort to wearing damp clothes or wearing our soiled clothes from the day before. I vividly remember attending school and being envious of my classmates wearing beautiful clothes. In the winter they would come to school appropriately attired in wool coats, scarves, mittens, and boots. I would look down at my holey, wet sneakers and feel my face become flushed from embarrassment. I was fortunate that my classmates did not tease me about the condition of my clothes. When we got home from school my siblings and I would run to the hot radiators for warmth. We would hang our socks on them and place our worn-out shoes or sneakers under them to dry. Other times we went to the laundromat to wash our clothes. We used so many washers and dryers. It seemed like it took forever. I could not wait for the day when I would no longer have to go to the laundromat. When Mama could afford it, she used a laundry man in town. This was very expensive for us. So many clothes to wash when you have that many children!

At times, due to lack of money, in the winter months our house was very cold. We could not afford to buy coal. When we could buy it, we would wait for the coal man to arrive with this special gold. When we did not have heat, Mama gathered all of us into the kitchen. She lit the stove and oven and we would huddle around it to keep warm. Yet, even when the house became warm, our bones retained the memory of coldness from the freezing days. I lived with the fear that I would never be warm enough or that we would run out of coal again. In fact, later on in life, the memory of the uncomfortable coldness caused me to keep my apartments and homes at higher temperatures than most people would tolerate. Even though logically I knew I had enough money to warm my home, the days of suffering from the cold still lived on inside me.

A shortage of food during the winter months was another problem we encountered. Mama made oatmeal in a huge aluminum pot. Standing around the stove, we would eagerly await her announcement that the oatmeal was ready. Oatmeal was the staple we ate for breakfast, lunch, and dinner. Sometimes there was only enough oatmeal for one meal. Sometimes there was not any food at all.

In school the aroma of the food cooking in the cafeteria was more than I could handle when I had no lunch money. I was starving and felt the hunger pangs in my stomach and longed to pick up a tray and indulge in even the worst tasting hot school lunches. Sometimes I would sit with the brown bag lunch kids and watch them take out a thick ham or peanut butter and jelly sandwich, a fresh orange, and a cupcake. When I did bring a sandwich to school, it was often a ketchup sandwich. To this day I can no longer eat ketchup. I do not even put it on French fries or hamburgers. I thought to myself that one day I would never hunger for food again. I am sure this caused me to have difficulty with food for the rest of my life.

As a young child I had gotten the nickname of "Carol the Barrel." At the time it caused me lots of pain. Despite the fact that I was an extremely active child I was still chubby compared to my siblings. Therefore, they constantly teased me. This was one more reason to feel bad about myself. However, I came to realize their teasing was not of a malicious nature. Once again it was just kids being kids.

Weight continues till this day to be an uphill battle for me. Later in life I was diagnosed as having hypothyroidism (underactive thyroid gland). Along with taking medicine I have dieted and exercised from time to time throughout my life. As a child I would walk to town which was approximately a mile away to meet my friends. I wasn't even aware that I was getting this exercise. Once I began to travel by car exercise became work instead of part of my daily life. Now walking has become my exercise of choice. I live near beautiful Rockland Lake where I try to walk a distance of three miles every day; this is where I was inspired to write my book.

Walking has led me to feeling good inside and looking better on the outside. There have been times when I have been thinner than I am now. Even though I was thin I didn't feel good about myself. Though I often received compliments about my appearance I never felt beautiful on the inside. I strived to be thin for the wrong reasons. I craved the attention from others and received it, but my need for attention was never satisfied. Along with being thin I dyed my hair blonde in my teen years, and this caused an amazing reaction to my looks. The invisible Carol appeared - on the outside at least.

Today I am at a point where I am at peace with who I am. It has taken all these years but I finally realize that I don't have to be thin to feel beautiful. I now appreciate the beauty within myself and my outer appearance has become secondary.

It was painful for Mama and Daddy to watch their children experience life without even the bare necessities at times. They did not choose for us to be poor. It was forced upon them because of the lace mill closings. My parents did the best they could under the circumstances. I imagine that our love for each other is what got us through these desperate times. While I am grateful love pulled us through these tough times, the need for money was a lesson I would never forget. Though I was just a little girl at the time, I knew even then that when I grew up I would strive to make sure that I would have a beautiful home and a rich life like those of my school friends. More importantly, I would make sure that my own children, if I were to have any, would be provided with the essentials of life.

CHAPTER TEN

MORE THAN JUST A HOUSE

After the construction of the Tappan Zee Bridge, many New York City residents moved to the suburbs seeking a better way of life for their families. The housing market could not keep up with the demand for houses required by the young families moving in by droves to the largest hamlet in Rockland. On Congers Road new developments with fabulous houses were springing up left and right.

When I was young and impressionable, I equated money with happiness. Thus, I assumed my friends and schoolmates were richer and happier than I was because they lived in big, beautiful houses. Across the street my good friend, Karen Cross, lived in one. I remember sitting on my bed and looking out the window at her house and dreaming that one day I would live in such a beautiful house. I would do whatever was necessary to make this happen. No longer would I want for the things that others had. Though my house was large, it was in dire need of repair. I was embarrassed to invite friends over. However, I did make exceptions for a few of my friends. The first year Karen moved into her house we became friends. Marvin and her brother Dick also became friends. Recently she shared with me that when Marvin and Dick were in third grade Dick had come over to play at our house. After Dick went home he told his mom that the people across the street were rich because they had a color TV and a four slice toaster. Since his family had neither of these things he thought we were rich!

Karen also mentioned that she still enjoys telling people that her neighbor from across the street was her school friend that came from a family of twenty children and there were no twins!

Another friend I invited to my house was Maureen Nevins. We knew each other from school, but it wasn't until I had an unfortunate accident that I learned Maureen was a person I could trust. When I was 13 years old, I walked barefoot about a mile to downtown New City to meet a friend, named Penny. I preferred walking in bare feet because I was embarrassed to wear my holey sneakers. We were playing in a building that was under construction. A dart sticking out of the ceiling caught my attention. I jumped up to get it and my right foot landed on a broken bottle. I cut my foot quite seriously. The cut was deep and blood was spurting out. I needed to get to the hospital immediately. Instead of waiting for an ambulance, a policeman drove me to the hospital. The doctor called my parents to tell them I needed surgery. I told the doctor Mama needed to hear my voice on the phone so she would know I was alive and okay. I knew she would think the worst if I didn't speak with her; he promptly granted my request. Daddy had come from work to the hospital to be by my side and to take me home after surgery. As a result of the operation I had to walk with crutches for a couple of months. Mama had a bed placed in the parlor for me because I couldn't walk up and down stairs. She nurtured me until my foot healed. While lying in bed I remembered when Judy's leg was hurt and all the attention she received. I was so jealous of her. I then realized all the attention wasn't worth all the pain. While I was at school someone had to carry my books to class for me. Maureen volunteered and we became close friends. I invited her to my house because I trusted her not to pass judgment on the poor condition of my house. She liked me for me; she was a true friend.

Our house had very large rooms and its layout still lingers in my mind. When you walked through the side door of the house (it was never locked) you entered the downstairs hallway. Its entire wall served as my canvas. It is where I aspired to become a great artist like Michelangelo. Though unappreciated by my parents, I was positive my scribbling was that of a great master, namely me. The only bathroom was situated off this hallway. Having one bathroom was problematic indeed! With so many of us sharing one bathroom everyone needed to get in and out as quickly as possible. "Hurry up, I gotta go!" was commonly yelled by someone standing outside the bathroom door. The toilet would break down because it was flushed so often. For as long as I can remember the shower was broken, so we took baths. We couldn't even take a bath when there wasn't any hot water. So many people used hot water that it took awhile for the water to reheat. We needed clean towels, toilet paper, tooth paste, toothbrushes, and shampoo for twelve of us.

In the dining room there was an oversized built-in hutch with glass doors and deep drawers. This hutch served as a showcase for our family's trophies and medals. When Mama greeted new visitors to the house she led them directly to the hutch and proudly expounded on which child earned which trophy, athletic letter, or medal. In one of the drawers Marvin's cat BeeBee birthed her kittens. This is especially memorable because it was on Marvin's 9th birthday that he opened the drawer and to his surprise found darling kittens snuggled up to BeeBee. He acted like the proud father! He and the rest of us were sure it was BeeBee's gift to him for his birthday. Fruits such as peaches and bananas were left to ripen in another drawer.

It was a huge dining room and a big dining table with its many unmatched chairs stood smack in the middle of it. No matter where we were in the house the delicious aromas of whatever Mama was cooking enticed us to the table. The chairs filled up quickly to ensure we got large portions of our favorite foods before they disappeared. For fear of not getting enough of my favorites, I shoveled the food in my mouth as fast as I could. In fact, I developed a life-long bad habit of eating my food as though I'm in a hurry. I'm regularly the person to finish eating my meal before anyone else. Sometimes this habit annoys others, and I don't enjoy watching others eat while I have nothing to do.

When Daddy wasn't working and could eat meals with us, he always sat at the head of the table. Daddy was a meat and potato man. He had to have bread and butter served with every meal. Mama's specially prepared savory gravy was the perfect sauce to pour over her hand-mashed potatoes and succulent roasts. Mealtime was one of the happiest times of the day! We chattered away while eating one of Mama's home cooked meals. It seems the tradition of families gathering around the table for dinner or any mealtime is quickly becoming a thing of the past. It's sad because a natural healthy bonding occurs when a family gathers together to share a home cooked meal and their thoughts. It certainly worked that way for our family.

Having Marvin's birthday parties in this room was very special. Marvin was Mama's last born so she doted on him the most. He was the only one I can remember who was given a huge birthday party. The rest of us knew this was a big deal! Neighborhood children were invited to the party, which had never happened before. Cousins and siblings attended as well. Crepe paper hung across the room. Everyone got a party bag with a hat and blower. Each child got a large vanilla and orange sherbet ice cream cup along with a piece of birthday cake. I'm sure Mama would have liked to have given each of her children a similar birthday party. It was simply impossible to do with so many children. However, she celebrated each of our birthdays with a birthday cake and ice cream. Surprisingly, Daddy knew the birthdates of every one of his children. After Mama died he would either give or mail a birthday card to us on our special day.

The dining room table was used for more than just eating meals! Sometimes we would lay a large piece of plywood across it, so it became a ping pong table. We had our very own tournaments. The ping pong ball bounced back and forth for hours as we competed against each other. I will never forget the laughter and fun I had with my sisters and brothers while playing this game. I never stopped to think that it might be better to have a recreation room or a real ping pong table. I was just a kid having a blast! When Marvin couldn't play basketball outside he found a way to do it inside. He had the dining room door opened up against the wall. He rolled up socks to make like they were a ball and would shoot at the space between the door and wall, using that space as a basket. I used to enjoy pitching baseball cards with my siblings against the walls. I was quite good at it.

At times the power would go off and my siblings and myself would all gather around the dining room table and sit by candle light. Bobby would tell us scary stories. We all enjoyed the stories and were always sad when the electricity came back on.

All windows were dressed with flowered, plastic curtains. I hated those plastic curtains! Mama bought the curtains at John's Bargain Store (it was similar to today's dollar stores). There were old worn out oak floors in our dining room and parlor covered with oilcloth, an inexpensive floor covering (Oilcloth was a common floor covering during the 1950's). Little did I know had we been able to refinish those floors they would have been beautiful, even by today's standards. The house had plaster-filled fireplaces in the dining room, living room, and two of the upstairs bedrooms. I had always wished they had been open so we could have enjoyed them.

Walk into the parlor and there sat Mama in her favorite chair, the heart of our home. Oh, how I miss those days of Judy and me sitting and snuggling on either side of Mama's lap while she sat in that huge, overstuffed green chair. She had that "motherly scent" and we felt there was no other place we would rather be. Immediately to the left of the chair was the brown cot – this was the recovery bed. Mama would hold and comfort all of her sick children here. She had such a loving way about her that made us feel so much better.

Not all memories of Mama sitting in her favorite chair are cheerful ones. When she became very displeased with one of us for misbehaving, like arguing with each other, she sometimes responded by grabbing a teacup or whatever object was resting on the end table, and throwing it at one or more of us. Usually it would just hit the parlor wall, and she would yell, "Look at what you made me do! Now clean up that mess." Mama's sense of justice did not always correspond with ours. It didn't matter who caused the problem. One of us had to clean it up, the culprit or not.

Sometimes Daddy would discipline us by telling us to go stand in the corner. Occasionally I would get uncontrollable giggles which aggravated him. So, once as punishment for doing this he told me to go stand in the corner. He completely forgot about me and left me there. It seemed like I was standing there for a very long time. Finally, I went to Daddy and asked if I could get out of the corner. Daddy let me know he felt bad and apologized for doing this.

They were strict disciplinarians and of the belief children should be seen and not heard. Though sometimes feeling burdened by the strict parenting, we felt loved, and also witnessed the love they had for each other. Each treated the other with respect and kindness. Pet names like "Honey" and "Dear" were often used. We were truly blessed to grow up in a home with parents who were truly in love.

The TV set was in the parlor as well. Daddy never bought himself anything and wanted a color TV. When they saved enough money Mama told Daddy to go buy it. Times were different back then and they sacrificed having a comfortable couch to buy the color TV. We felt like we were rich being the proud owners of a "color" TV set, especially since they were so expensive when they first came out! Some shows were still in black and white - that's how new color programming was to television. There were no remotes! We had to get up off the couch or the floor to change a TV station. After working all week Daddy would lie on the couch and watch TV. He especially enjoyed watching westerns like "Gunsmoke" and "Bonanza." "The Little Rascals" and "The Three Stooges" were two of my favorites. Sometimes we watched TV shows together. "Lassie" was one show I remember in particular.

Mama and Daddy instilled in us a great sense of fun. They never lost their love of dancing. Marvin, Judy, and I had vivid memories of how they gracefully waltzed around the parlor to the music of The Lawrence Welk TV show. Being just little kids, we would giggle. Yet, even at such a young age we appreciated and enjoyed their wonderful talent and display of affection. When I got older Daddy tried to teach me how to waltz but I had difficulty learning to dance. My brothers, Marvin and Bobby, were the ones who inherited their talent for dancing.

We sisters often sneaked off with one another's clothes. Sometimes we couldn't find a clean outfit of our own to wear, so we just took another sister's. It was usually without their knowledge. Ruthie shared these few stories with me. Once, she took Linda's brown skirt and a flowered orange and white shirt and threw them out Annie's bedroom window. Then she would go down stairs and get the clothes. She got dressed in Linda's clothes in the mud room. She had to hurry to catch the school bus before Linda left for school. The reason she got away without Linda seeing her in school dressed in her clothes was because she was in eighth grade and Linda was in ninth so their paths never crossed. Another time, she wore a nice shirt of Linda's and some guy at school thought he was being funny and pulled the fairy loop on the shirt, ripping the shirt. Linda never saw that shirt again! Also, Annie had a particularly pretty white shirt that she borrowed and wore to school and some guy thought he was being funny and sprayed blue ink on it. Annie never saw that shirt again! Needless to say, if our sisters found out we took their clothes there would have been a lot of sibling arguing going on.

When I wasn't taking my sisters clothes I usually wore their hand-me-down clothes. I only got new clothes for Easter, my birthday, beginning of the school year, and Christmas.

It was when our family filled these rooms with laughter and love that it became a "home." Mama and Daddy had close relationships with their siblings. We all would be so thrilled when they came to visit. Especially when Mama's brother, Uncle Charlie came to visit. He played his guitar, harmonica, and sang songs for our family. It was so much fun to hear Mama laughing and enjoying herself. There were to be many wonderful times in this house.

CHAPTER ELEVEN

MERRY CHRISTMAS!

Christmas time was the highlight of the year for the Hampson Family. We always had the most beautiful live Christmas trees. Daddy usually picked out and bought our tree. When Bobby was old enough he would go out to buy it. The tree had to be as tall as the ceiling and as full and wide as it could be! I can still remember the lovely, fresh scent of pine when it was brought into the house. Mama would always say how beautiful the tree was and get so excited. There was nothing like pleasing Mama and seeing that smile on her face! Bobby basked in Mama's praise of his having found the perfect tree.

Daddy was in charge of decorating the tree. The tree had to be decorated just so. A star on top went on first, then the strands of lights, pretty ornaments, and garland. My siblings would make paper chains that were hung on the tree. The tinsel was the biggest deal of all because it had to look just perfect! Daddy taught me that you had to have patience putting on the tinsel. It went on strand by strand. The tree had a radiant glow when you looked at it. Later on in life, when looking for a Christmas tree, I would always try to find a tree that was as beautiful as our childhood tree.

Mama and Daddy would host a Christmas Eve party with my adult siblings, their spouses, and a couple of their friends. I think this started because my siblings spent Christmas Day with their spouses' families. My sisters and I would clean up the house and help get ready for the party. Mama made roast beef, baked ham, and egg potato salad. Pauline brought homemade pork pies and a lemon meringue pie (Daddy's favorites). Marlon brought baked beans and shrimp macaroni salad. Mama put ribbon candy and peanut brittle out on the table. Highballs were the drink of the night.

As gifts Mama and Daddy would give all the guys a bottle of liquor and the women would get a box of chocolates.

No children were allowed at the Christmas Eve party. So Judy, Ruthie and I would sit on the hallway stairs listening to the party going on. Ruthie remembered we watched everyone come in with presents for us. We would be giggling and get so excited! One of us would say that's a big box! Who is it for? Of course, it was always for Marvin because he was the baby! We could hear all the laughter and fun they were having. I wanted so much to be at the party. Later on that night when the party was over I would sneak downstairs to see all my presents. Wow! All the presents that were under the tree were unbelievable! You can't even imagine what it looked like. Sometime in the night I couldn't stand having to wait for Christmas, so I sneaked downstairs and opened most of my presents to see what I had gotten. Then I rewrapped them. I found out later in life Ruthie was doing the same thing and still did as an adult. Mama knew we were doing this and told us we would be sorry because we wouldn't have anything to open up on Christmas Day. She was right.

On Christmas Day it was like heaven on earth! Judy, Ruthie, and I woke up and slid down the banister! Spending time with my siblings and the opening of all the presents was so exciting! I usually got the necessities such as pajamas, underwear, and socks. I always loved getting a new doll and a few toys. The smell of the huge turkey roasting in the oven filled the house for hours. Mama would make a wonderful turkey dinner with all the trimmings. We all sat around the table enjoying her cooking and being together. Later in life, Ruthie informed me it was now my responsibility to have a Christmas Eve party because I lived in

New York, and the family should get together for Christmas. Thus, we started the tradition of hosting the parties in our home. It was Peter's idea to dress up as Santa to entertain the children. This became another tradition that was passed on down to our family. Marvin and Mary Ellen would take turns having a Christmas Eve party at their home. After she was married we passed down that honor to Bobby's daughter Rachel and her husband Dom. Bobby would be so very proud to know his daughter is carrying on the family tradition. This tradition is now shared amongst Erica and her cousins. Christmas became a huge part of the niece's and nephew's relationship with each other and their aunts and uncles. We came to realize it was my family being together that made our Christmases so special. Gift giving was simply a part of the festivities. Without the love Christmas would not have held its special place in our lives!

CHAPTER TWELVE

WE ALL LOOK ALIKE

Everywhere I went I was recognized as a Hampson. "Are you Judy or Carol? Which Hampson are you?" These were common questions asked of us when greeted by friends and strangers alike. I was proud to be recognized as a Hampson, although, at the same time I was disappointed that they did not realize right away that "I am Carol." People would say "You could always tell a Hampson when you see one," a common remark we always heard. We had a striking family resemblance to each other yet we were all individuals with our own personalities.

The reason that we were so proud to be identified as a Hampson was because our family was so well-respected. The high academic successes and athletic successes of so many children in one family led others to hold us in high regard.

However, another response from people was shock that there were so many children in my family. OMG twenty! Holy crap! You come from a family of 20? Some people didn't really believe I was one of twenty children so they asked me to name all of us (I would have to explain what happened to my siblings that had died.) Being the second to the youngest it was difficult remembering so many siblings' names. I wasn't able to learn their names in the correct birth order. While growing up I felt sometimes we weren't a family of sixteen. It was as though we had three separate families in one family. The youngest five;

Marvin, Carol, Judy, Ruthie, and Linda were one family. The next five; David, Bobby, Jesse, Annie, and Charlie. Then the oldest; Roy, Inez, Donald, Harry, Eddie, and Edith. Other times it was as though we were one family. When any of us would talk with one of our siblings we always asked how the others were doing. It was understood that no matter what time of day or night, if any one of us needed help, one of us would be there. There was strength in numbers and a loving bond between us. Until this day we are constantly barraged by questions from people. Are there any twins? Are they from the same parents? Did any of us have a large family like what we came from? If they didn't was it because it was difficult being so poor, economic reasons, or something else? The most children any of my siblings had was four. I don't know the reasons as to why they didn't have large families. God has blessed us with a beautiful healthy daughter. I wanted another child, but I suffered an ectopic pregnancy, a pregnancy in which the fetus developed in my fallopian tube. I had emergency surgery. Sometime later I had a miscarriage and decided to no longer try to have any more children. I didn't want a large family because I believed parents shouldn't have more children than they can afford. Also, it wasn't the lifestyle that I wanted to live.

These questions can be hard to respond to at times because while they find it surprising, it is an accepted norm in my family. To us it is no different than them coming from a small family. Being from such an unusually large family caused me, at times, to feel like a social misfit. It was not until we had the second family reunion in 2002 that I personally understood what made me feel this way. It was when I held the custom-made tee shirts in my hands and saw a list of our names in black and white that I personally had a response of "Wow, I'm from an abnormally large family!" When I showed people the tee shirts a reaction that I received was to put an announcement about the family reunion in our local newspaper. One of the explanations they gave as why they thought it should be in the paper was because they thought that the story of such a remarkable family reunion should be shared. The fact that so many brothers and sisters traveled across the country to come together for a family reunion would be of special interest to others.

However, I didn't want to share my family with the community. While I was proud of being a member of this family reunion, I didn't want our family on display for people to read about as though we were a sideshow at a circus. Yet why am I writing about our family now? When I was a child a man came to our house and wanted to write a story about our family. Our parents told him they weren't interested. I have been told Mama and Daddy wouldn't like our family story told. I have asked myself if I am doing the right thing. Appreciating that our story should be told by one of the twenty, I decided to do it. In 2010 when I started writing my story there were fourteen living children. As of November, 2018 there are only six of us left.

CHAPTER THIRTEEN

SCHOOL, SPORTS & SUCCESS

New City Elementary was less than a mile from my house. Classwork and homework were becoming more difficult every year. When I was in fourth grade, David tutored me after school because of my failing grades. He wanted so much for me to be a better student. In spite of his help I did fail and had to repeat fourth grade. School was boring and sitting still at my desk was nearly impossible. This caused problems with my teacher. I have had difficulty memorizing throughout my life. Keeping a child back in school is not always the answer. It was not the answer for me. Every child is an individual and learns at different rates. Now I would tell my fourth grade self just because someone got straight A's in school doesn't mean they were smart in everything. Academically smart doesn't mean they are good at managing their personal lives. Don't compare yourself to anyone. Just be happy with who you are.

Most of my brothers and sisters excelled in academics and some had brilliant minds. Receiving high grades was an expectation set by Daddy, which most of them lived up to. Living up to these standards contributed to believing that failing was shameful and led to my low self esteem.

Felix V. Festa Junior High School was next. I wanted to escape my academic problems. Interest in boys and being popular were more important than grades then, and also helped build up my self-esteem. Most of the time in class was spent writing notes to my friends and boyfriend. In ninth grade I ran for class secretary and simply thought of it as a popularity contest. In spite of my stage fright I delivered my campaign speech to the student body in the auditorium. Although not qualified for the position, I won. The minutes of the class meetings had to be taken down and then relayed over the loud speaker for all to hear. I had gotten in over my head and therefore struggled doing the job. In tenth grade I went to Clarkstown Senior High School (later known as Clarkstown North). The school was just up the street, close enough to walk to. Many of my brothers and sisters had gone there before me, so my belief was that the teachers expected me to be as smart as they were. In 1973, although school had been difficult, graduation and a high school diploma was achieved. Hooray! It was my senior class that split up and would have two graduating classes; Clarkstown High School North and Clarkstown High School South.

While talking with Annie recently she shared that she was grateful for Daddy's love and direction wanting all his children to graduate high school. All sixteen children graduated (Marvin, Carol, Judy, Ruthie, Linda, Bobby, David, Jesse, Annie, and Charlie from Clarkstown High School and Roy, Inez, Donald, Harry, Eddie, and Edith in Rhode Island), which is quite an impressive accomplishment! Most of them furthered their education after that.

Harry received his master's degree in science education from Columbia University. I loved telling everyone my brother graduated from an Ivy League school. Roy earned a bachelor's degree in civil engineering at the University of Rhode Island and some post-graduate work at the University of California, Los Angeles. He worked many years for the state of California. From 1973 to 1986 he was an executive officer of the Lahontan Regional Water Quality Board. In 1986, he opened his own consulting business, Roy C. Hampson & Associates. Throughout my life, Roy always made me feel like I was special. For most of our lives he lived in California while I resided in New York. Despite the long distance between us, our close bond remained intact. He never married or had any children. His dedication as an Environmental Civil Engineer became the main focus of his life. I was a mature married woman when Roy died, and it was Donald and I who traveled to his home in Lake Tahoe to make his funeral arrangements. Linda received a master's degree in English education from Virginia Commonwealth University. Judy received a master's degree in elementary education with a minor in reading from the University of North Florida. I attended Rockland Community College in Suffern, New York and majored in Computer Science.

Four of my siblings had careers as teachers. Others also went on to have very successful careers. David wrote a book, a collection of short stories called "The Bright Side of Life." Ruthie, Linda, and David all enjoyed writing poetry. Linda and David have published a few of their poems. Ruthie wrote a beautiful poem for her siblings about what it's like to be one of sixteen. Unfortunately, she had passed on before she published her poem.

Another expectation of Daddy was that all his children excel in sports. Besides academics my siblings were talented athletes. The Hampson brothers made sports headlines in their local newspapers as star athletes, some of them excelling in more than one sport.

Eight of my brothers became acquainted with golf by caddying and soon developed into accomplished golfers. They won tournaments and championships. Harry began caddying at age 12 at local country clubs. This was where he learned to play golf. At age 17, he won the New England Junior Golf Championship and the Northeast Jaycees Golf Tournament. He qualified and competed at the National Junior Golf Championship in Eugene, Oregon. "HARRY HAMPSON WINS NEW ENGLAND HEARST JR. TOURNEY" was just one example of the Rhode Island newspaper headlines about Harry.[4] Growing up I would often see one or more brothers

---

[4] Smith, Ambrose R. "Harry Hampson Wins New England Hearst Jr. Tourney." *Pawtuxet Valley Daily Times* [West Warwick, RI], 23 July 1952. Hampson Family Archives.

swinging a golf club in our yard! David tried to teach me to play. If my brothers weren't golfing they were playing football, basketball or track at school. Daddy was a fine athlete who played football and ran track in high school. He wanted his sons to follow in his footsteps. David, Bobby, Jesse and Charlie were all outstanding runners for Clarkstown Senior High School. One article stated "Jesse Hampson turned in the best time of the day in leading the Rams to a second straight cross country win of the '63 season".[5] David was one of the premier distance runners in Rockland County from 1963-1967. On June 4, 2007 he was inducted into the Clarkstown North High School "Sports Hall of Fame."

Marvin was a star athlete, thus "Marvelous Marv." When he was younger he played Little League Baseball. The field was close to our home. Mama would tell me to go down to the field and watch his games to make sure he was okay and to support him. I enjoyed watching him play. I think this is where my interest for cheerleading began. In high school Marvin became a great basketball player.

Sports was another area in which I tried to live up to Daddy's expectations. Even to this day I can feel the high that I felt when I was an athlete in New City Elementary. In gym we would play dodgeball, and I was usually the last one standing. It wasn't until playing in extramural activities that I met up with tougher competition. This was where I faced the fact that I couldn't win with natural ability alone. I couldn't handle not being the best. I took the easy route out and simply lost interest to avoid losing. I still participated in sports but it never held the same level of excitement.

From September 1970 to June 1971 I was a Junior Varsity Cheerleader for Clarkstown Senior High School and Judy was a Varsity cheerleading alternate. Why did I want to become a cheerleader? To be popular and the center of attention. I wanted to be noticed in a family of sixteen as doing something great. I

---

[5] "Rams, Taps Mounties Record Harrier Wins." *The Rockland County Journal - News* [Nyack, NY], 27 September 1963, p. 25. Hampson Family Archives.

worked very hard and practiced every day in my driveway until tryouts. My hard work paid off and I made it! Ruthie was so proud of me becoming a cheerleader she bought me my cheerleading coat. In September 1971 I made Junior Varsity cheerleading again and was Co-Captain. I cheered for awhile and later decided to not continue to be a cheerleader as I wanted to spend more time with my boyfriend. In high school I also played intramural soccer and extramural basketball. Judy, Ruthie, and Linda all lettered in various varsity sports in high school. Judy went on to play field hockey and basketball at SUNY Oneonta.

It was impossible for Mama to display all her children's trophies, medals, and school letters. The massive amount of awards resulted not only because of the large number of children, but also due to the fact that each child was so talented that each received many awards.

CHAPTER FOURTEEN

TILL DEATH US DO PART

In January 1971 Mama was enthusiastically planning their 40th wedding anniversary party. She never lived to celebrate this milestone. Sadly, one day Mama became ill and an ambulance came to our house and took her to Nyack Hospital. While she was there I was planning to attend a school dance. She requested that she see me before I went so she could see me all dressed up. When I stood before her she told me I looked beautiful. As sick as she was she still cared about how I looked and made me feel so loved and special.

While having a hernia operation the doctors discovered she had ovarian cancer that had metastasized. She was always fearful if they ever opened her up for surgery they would find cancer. Her worst fear had come true. The doctor told Daddy she didn't have long to live. Though they were heartbroken they knew they would have to tell all their children the news.

While she was in the hospital Daddy had to be admitted into the hospital as well to have cataract surgery. Mama insisted she wanted to be close to her husband's room. Since there was no room available near him they wheeled her bed down the hall and left her outside his room so she could be close to him. This was true love. Mama and Daddy loved each other right till the end! Mama passed away on January 28, 1971, at the age of 55, which happened to be the anniversary date of her deceased nine year old son Roland's birthday.

I was sixteen and Marvin was thirteen when she died. Daddy requested we all wear black to her funeral. Our grieving family was photographed in our dining room. It was the only time a photograph of all sixteen children was ever taken. More photos were taken of Mama laid out in her coffin at the funeral home. I decided to hold on to them for other generations to keep. For many it was a most inspiring sight to see all sixteen of us together at her funeral. People spoke very highly of her and recognized how she was so loved by her children. Life wasn't the same after Mama died. It was difficult to live without her in our lives. After she died rarely did anyone come to visit us.

We (Marvin, Carol, Judy, Ruthie, Bobby, Jesse, Annie and Daddy) moved and leased a tiny house on Wyndham Lane in New City. Eventually Marvin, Jesse, Daddy and I would be the last ones living in the house. After graduating high school, I soon wanted my independence and moved out. Later on I had moved to Belen, New Mexico and lived with Bobby, his wife Lorraine, and family. After a few months I moved to San Diego, California and lived with David, his wife Noel, and family. While I was living in San Diego, Daddy had a stroke in New York. I was so upset that I decided to move back home to make sure Daddy was okay. He never was the same after Mama died and his health was getting worse. One day while working at the court house he fell ill and came home from work early. Jesse and I took him to the hospital. He had gone into a diabetic coma. Daddy passed away on February 14, 1977 at the age of 64. We were all heartbroken again. Daddy was a well-liked and well-respected man while working for the County of Rockland. On February 15, 1977, there was a Rockland County Legislature meeting. The meeting was adjourned in memory of Daddy. There were many kind words said about him.

Some of us believed because Daddy died on Valentine's Day it was due to a broken heart. It gave us comfort to think that God called him to heaven to join Mama on this day of love. For several years after I had a difficult time celebrating Valentine's Day. In time I would choose to celebrate this holiday for love once again.

Jesse had always helped support our household and continued even after Daddy died. In many ways he had become a father figure to Marvin and me. Once Marvin, Jesse and I had moved out of the house we no longer had a family home where we could go to share our joys and sorrows with each other.

We all knew eventually we would have to experience the pain of losing each other to death. It was the price we would pay for being from this large family with so much love.

It wasn't until I grew up and got married that I fully appreciated what a unique love Mama and Daddy shared. Later on in life many of us realized that they were a tough act to follow. We learned from them that marriage is a sacred bond to be cherished for a lifetime. The power of love between Mama and Daddy was unlike any other I have ever seen. They were so young when they fell in love, and yet, it was the strength of their love that sustained them through life's tragedies. It was this same love that allowed them to move past hard times and embrace hopes of a better future. I have no doubt that Mama's and Daddy's teachings will live on for generations to come.

Will anyone ever KNOW
What it's like to be one of sixteen?
To have so many brothers and sisters
And the love between.

To share what little there is
And rejoice in what we give.
If only for a moment
The love will be seen.

Though we're miles apart
The love never stops.
Flowing like a river
Through everyone's heart.

For each of us it's different
With many memories shared.
But always knowing
There's someone who always cared.

We're separate people
Each of us.
Looking so much alike
You'd always KNOW a HAMPSON
On first sight.

We've added to our family.
Now we're all adults.
To know it was NOT the HOUSE
But the HOME.

We must keep alive the feelings
That MOM AND DAD BESTOWED
For in each of us
Is part of them
Which needs time to grow.

RUTH HAMPSON HRICKO

ACKNOWLEDGMENTS

I am deeply grateful to my sister, Linda Hampson Smedley, for her invaluable contributions to the creation of my memoir. Without her excellent editing, this book never would have been finished.

Special thanks to my other living siblings, Inez Craig, Annie Davis, Charlie Hampson, Judith Robinson, and to my siblings who contributed before passing on, David Hampson, Donald Hampson, Jesse Hampson, Marvin Hampson, Ruth Hricko, for their input and believing that I would do my best to consider everyone's feelings.

I wish to acknowledge with gratitude their awesome support while writing my memoir: Robin Craig, Jennifer Davis-Greene, Doug Hampson, Kevin Hampson, Roland Hampson, Carolyn Hricko, Suzanne Mackey, Dina McDaniel, Jim Smedley, and Laura Tangen.

To my brother-in-law, Richard Robinson, for his extraordinary feedback and proofreading my book. For her great creative design, I would like to thank my niece, Crystal Rothhaar, for the front and back cover.

To Brian Greene, I offer my sincere appreciation for your helpful comments and wise counsel.

I owe my heartfelt gratitude to my daughter, Erica Tobin, and my son-in-law, John for their encouragement and wonderful support along the way. I love you with all my heart!

Most of all, I want to thank my husband, Peter, for reviewing the story and giving me advice. You saw me through it till the end and I couldn't have done it without you. It was great working with you.

Many thanks to the following people for their support: Heather Anne, Dick Cross, Karen Cross, Susie Delo, Keith Henderson, Charlotte O'Connell, Maureen Shea, John Tobin, and Paula Tobin.

In memory of my parents, Harold and Inez Hampson, and my siblings who left this world way to soon. I love and miss you.

ABOUT THE AUTHOR

Carol Vislocky (née Hampson) is the nineteenth child of Inez and Harold Hampson. When her Grandpa Ted came to visit they would sit on the front porch and he would lovingly share stories about his life growing up in England. She did not pay much attention back then, and is so sorry for that. As an adult she wished he had written those stories down. Carol believes this is when a seed was planted for the writing of her memoir.

She is a wife, mom, and a proud grandma. She attended Rockland Community College in Suffern, New York and majored in Computer Science. Carol enjoys being with her grandchildren, taking walks, playing blackjack, and going to the beach.

In 2010, when she started writing her story, there were fourteen living children. As of November, 2018 there are only six left. Carol, her husband Peter, and cat live in New City, New York.

Made in the USA
Columbia, SC
17 September 2022